The True Story of the Hatfield and McCoy Feud

The True Story of the Hatfield and McCoy Feud

L.D. HATFIELD

NEW YORK

The True Story of the Hatfield and McCoy Feud First published in 1944. Current edition published by Cosimo Classics in 2012.

Cover copyright © 2012 by Cosimo, Inc. Cover design by www.popshopstudio.com Cover image © Jupiterimages Corporation, #19353933.

ISBN: 978-1-61640-747-6

This edition is a classic text and may be considered rare. As such, it is possible that some of the text might be blurred or of reduced print quality. Thank you for your under-standing and we wish you a pleasant reading experience.

Cosimo aims to publish books that inspire, inform, and engage readers worldwide. We use innovative print-on-demand technology that enables books to be printed based on specific customer needs. This approach eliminates an artificial scarcity of publications and allows us to distribute books in the most efficient and environmentally sustainable manner. Cosimo also works with printers and paper manufacturers who practice and encourage sustainable forest management, using paper that has been certified by the FSC, SFI, and PEFC whenever possible.

Ordering Information:
Cosimo publications are available at online bookstores. They may also be purchased for educational, business, or promotional use:
Bulk orders: Special discounts are available on bulk orders for reading groups, organizations, businesses, and others.
Custom-label orders: We offer selected books with your customized cover or logo of choice.

For more information, contact us at:

Cosimo, Inc.
P.O. Box 416, Old Chelsea Station
New York, NY 10011
info@cosimobooks.com
www.cosimobooks.com

Mouth of Blackberry Creek

T HE above picture was taken from the West Virginia side
of Tug River, about one mile east of Matewan, West
Virginia, looking across into the mouth of Blackberry
Creek in Pike County, Kentucky. About three miles up this
creek near the old home of the Reverend Anderson Hatfield
is the scene of the beginning of the famous Hatfield and
McCoy feud which started on the first Monday in August in
the year of 1882.

There have been several versions written of this widely
known altercation between the two prominent mountain families, but no two of them have coincided as to the facts concerning a feud which has become nationally and even inter-
nationally known throughout the years, since these two clans

This is a picture of Lark McCoy who lived at Phelps, Ky., at the time of the feud. He did not take a leading part in the feud but was a brother of Randall McCoy, the actual feudal leader on the McCoy side.

stalked each other in the wilderness recesses of Tug River, along the borders of West Virginia and Kentucky which were at that time very sparsely settled.

It has been commonly rumored that the feud actually started because of a dispute between the two clans over the ownership of a hog. This, however, is not true. It is true that there had been some trouble in this respect prior to the actual beginning of the feud, but a more or less satisfactory settlement had been made concerning the hog.

In those days there were vast uninhabited tracts of land in this section of West Virginia and Kentucky covered by dense forest which afforded an unsurmountable amount of mast upon which the hogs of various settlers would feast during that particular season of the year.

Each settler would have a certain mark by which his hogs could be recognized from those of his neighbors. These marks would be cut in the ears of the hogs by their owners with the keen-bladed knife of the frontiersman by cutting what was known as the swallow-fork in the left ear; an upper-cut in the right ear, or perhaps an underbit in one ear and some other mark in the other ear and each settler would have a different mark.

When the acorns and other nuts from the native trees in the forest began to drop in the fall of the year, the settlers would drive their hogs into these woodland areas and leave them for weeks and months so that they might grow and

7

This is a picture of Bud McCoy. He was the son of Randall McCoy and participated in many pitched battles between the two clans. He came to his death fighting heroically for the principals he believed in.

fatten on the nuts, and when the time came to round up the hogs each settler would know his hogs by these markings.

The late Captain Anderson Hatfield, having received a captain's commission during his service in the Civil War and later most generally known as "Devil Anse" Hatfield, lived at Delorme, on the West Virginia side of Tug River about five miles above Matewan, West Virginia, in what was then Logan County but later became Mingo County. "Devil Anse" was also recognized as the leader of the feud on the Hatfield side. Randolf McCoy, the feudal leader on the McCoy side, lived on a tributary of Pond Creek in Pike County, Kentucky.

Between the homes of these two families was a vast, densely wooded section of several miles in which no one lived, and in this region roamed the hogs of both the Hatfields and the McCoys together with the hogs of several other mountain families who used this section as a range. Some of this land belonged to the McCoys and some to the Hatfields but there was no fence or other barrier to separate the two tracts, therefore the hogs of the two families had free range over the entire region and mingled together during the season.

On one occasion at round-up time the Hatfields brought in one hog with theirs that had no markings of any kind in its ears which would determine the owner. The McCoys found out about the Hatfields bringing in this hog that had no markings and they claimed it as their own and the Hatfields disputed their claim. The matter was settled in the Magistrate's

9

Court and it was decided that the Hatfields had a legal right to the hog since it bore no markings of any kind which would give the McCoys or anyone else the right to claim the hog.

This incident is possibly the cause of the many rumors being circulated that the feud between the two families started over a hog. Although the matter was settled in the Magistrate's Court there may have been ill feelings between the two factions and the ill feelings of those hardy pioneers were seldom forgotten and most usually handed down from one generation to another.

Both the Hatfields and McCoys originally came from England and settled in Virginia. In later years they drifted westward and possibly were among the first settlers of South Western Virginia in what is now known as Russell, Wise and Dickinson Counties.

Captain Anderson Hatfield, whom we will call "Devil Anse" in this story, was the son of Ephraim Hatfield and Nancy Vance Hatfield. He married Nancy Vance, the granddaughter of Elder Abner Vance of near Abingdon, Virginia. There is a story connected with Elder Abner Vance which is quite interesting:

During the early part of the eighteenth century Elder Abner Vance lived in the Clinch River Valley near Abingdon, Virginia. He was a minister in the old Primitive Baptist Church which is also known as the Hardshell, or Old Regular Baptist Church.

10

He was of quiet disposition and devoted to his family and friends. Also he was a frontiersman and hardy pioneer. He spent his time tending his crops, hunting and fishing and also ministering to the wants and needs of his family and preaching to his little flocks scattered over the sparsely settled country.

In his family was a grown daughter, who was the pride of the father's heart and home. In the vicinity lived a Dr. Horton who made love to this daughter and induced her to run away with him to be married. Instead of marrying her as he had promised, he kept her away for some time and debauched her. Having accomplished his hellish purpose he took her back one day to her father's door while the family were sitting at the dinner table. Calling the father's attention to his daughter's return he haughtily and sneeringly used the most heartless, cruel and vulgar language ever addressed by a seducer to a father about his daughter.

Elder Abner Vance, stung and driven to desperation by the insult, reached for his trusted rifle which hung in a rack over the door. Horton rode quickly away but stopped to let his horse drink in the ford of Clinch River about one hundred and seventy-five yards from Vance's house. While wating for his horse to drink, with his back to the house, Vance, who had gotten his gun, walked to the door, took deliberate aim and fired. The leaden missile fired by the unerring aim of the frontier preacher struck Horton in the back of his head, killing him instantly.

His horse had nearly reached the opposite bank before the

11

rider fell from his back into the river, from which he was later taken by his brother, Dan Horton. To this day that ford of the river is known as Horton's Ford.

After the shooting the Elder Vance bade a hasty farewell to his wife and children and shouldering his trusty rifle, started for security in the fastness of the almost trackless wilderness along the Tug and Guyan Rivers on the eastern border of Kentucky and the southern border of West Virginia. This region later became the permanent home of the Vances and Hatfields as well as the McCoys and others who migrated into the then new country.

The Elder Vance remained here for several years as a fugitive from the law. While here thus isolated as a fugitive and away from his family, he located and acquired several tracts of land containing many thousands of acres along Tug River on the borders of Kentucky and West Virginia and on Guyan River and Twelve-pole Creek in what is now Mingo and Logan Counties.

After several years of this isolated life and feeling that he was justified in the eyes of God and should be before any human tribunal for taking the life of one who had seduced his daughter, ruined the happiness of his home, and then taunted him with the most obscene epithets known to our language, he returned to his home and surrendered himself to the authorities. He was placed in jail and soon after put on trial for murder.

12

But alas, for him, one hundred years ago the unwritten law, the sanctity of the home, the purity and virtue of a daughter did not seem to be recognized as they are today. At least it seemed that way to him for he was given a hasty trial, convicted and sentenced to be hanged, because as they had reasoned, he had shot Horton in the back of the head.

The following song was written by him while in jail awaiting his execution and he sang this song on the gallows on the day he was hanged.

The Johnson referred to in the song was the judge who presided at his trial and McFarland was the prosecuting attorney. The Elliott referred to was a member of the jury which convicted the Elder Vance. This same Elliott had formerly been tried for murder in this same county and on that occasion the Elder Vance was a member of the jury which tried him. At the trial of Elliott the jury stood eleven for conviction but the Elder Vance did not believe him guilty as charged. He hung the jury for several days and finally won them over and they returned a verdict of not guilty. The same Elliott was said to have been the most damaging, relentless and vindicative witness and juryman against the Elder Vance.

THE SONG

Green grows the woods where Sandy flows,
And peace along its rills;
In the valley the black bear lies secure,
The red buck roves the hills.

But Vance no more shall Sandy behold,
Nor drink of its crystal wave;
The partial Judge pronounced his doom—
To the hunter a felon's grave

The Judge called me "incarnate fiend,"
For Eliott's life I saved;
I couldn't agree to Elliott's guilt,
Humanity belongs to the brave.

The mercy that I to others have shown,
Has never been shown to me;
Humanity, I say, belongs to the brave,
And I hope it belongs to me.

'Twas by advice of McFarland
Judge Johnson did me call;
I was taken from my native home,
And placed in yon stone wall.

My persecutors have gained their quest
Their promise to make good;
They often swore they'd never rest
Till they had my life's blood.

Daniel Horton, Bob and Bill,
A lie against me swore;
In order to take my life away,
That I should be no more.

But they and I together must meet,
Where all things are made known;
And if I shed a human's blood,
There'll mercy be me shown.

Bright shines the sun on Clinch's hills,
And soft the west wind blows;
The valleys are covered o'er with bloom,
Perfumed by the fragrant rose.

But Vance no more shall Sandy behold,
Nor smell the sweet perfume;
This day his eyes will close in death,
His body laid in the tomb.

Farewell my friends, my children dear,
To you I bid farewell;
The love I have for your precious souls,
No mortal tongue can tell.

Farewell to you my loving wife,
To you I bid adieu;
And if I reach fair Canaan's shore
I'll wait and watch for you.

Before his execution, which occurred about the year of 1800, the Elder Vance divided the lands which he had acquired during the time he was a fugitive among his children and they later settled in this section of Kentucky and West Virginia. One of his granddaughters, Nancy Vance, married Ephraim Hatfield and was the mother of "Devil Anse" Hatfield and several other children. Jim Vance, another of his grandchildren, was later an active participant in the Hatfield and McCoy feud.

To show the intensity of the feeling existing in the family some seventy-five years after the death of the Elder Vance, the following will illustrate:

Some thirty years ago a man rode up to the residence of Crocket Harrison, in Logan County, late in the evening and called at the gate. Mrs. Harrison, who was a Vance before her marriage and also a granddaughter of Abner Vance, answered the call and asked what he wanted. He told her he wished to stay over night as it was getting very late.

"What is your name? she asked.

"My name is Horton", he replied.

"God bless you, my name is Vance," she said, "and you can ride on."

The actual feud between these two families started on the first Monday in August in the year of 1882. It was the custom in those days to hold state and county elections at that time

16

of the year, and since election time was such an important event everyone wanted to be present, for then they could hear all the news and see all their friends from miles around, and possibly enjoy a little nip of the favorite nectar brewed by the light of the moon in those mountain recesses and carried in the well known "Little Brown Jug." Then it was no uncommon sight to meet your fellowman toting his jug, supported by a rope or cord around his neck, from which he could sip at leisure without removing the rope from over his head.

The election on this memorable occasion was being held under a large beech tree about three miles from the mouth of Blackberry Creek and near the home of the Reverend Anderson Hatfield, who was an election officer on this day. The Reverend Anderson Hatfield was a pioneer mountain preacher in the Old Regular Baptist Church and he was a cousin of "Devil Anse" Hatfield. To distinguish between these two Hatfields, who had the same name, may have had something to do with the clan leader being known as "Devil Anse." They were great friends and loved each other devotedly.

Ellison Hatfield and Elias Hatfield, both of them being brothers of "Devil Anse," lived on the West Virginia side of Tug River near Matewan. They had come that day to attend the election. This Elias Hatfield was the father of Dr. H. D. Hatfield, now of Huntington, West Virginia.

Ellison Hatfield married Sarah Staton and she had two brothers named Bill and John. Sometime prior to this date

17

three of Randolf McCoy's boys, Floyd, Tolbert and Richard (Dick), had been over in West Virginia and had some trouble with these two Staton boys and Bill Staton was killed by the McCoys.

Wall Hatfield, another brother of "Devil Anse," was then justice of the peace in Mingo County and these McCoys were brought before him for an examining trial for killing Bill Staton. The evidence proved that Staton had fired first on the McCoys and the McCoys had fired in self defense, killing Staton.

Ellison Hatfield, being a brother-in-law of Bill Staton, did all he could to convict the McCoys, but for lack of incriminating evidence the justice of the peace and brother of Ellison allowed them to go free.

These McCoys never liked Ellison Hatfield after he had tried so hard to prosecute them for killing his brother-in-law and they often made threats that they would take care of him.

These three McCoys together with their father, Randolf McCoy, were also present at the election on this date and it has been reliably stated that before coming to the election they sharpened their knives so as to be in readiness for Ellison Hatfield whom they expected to be present.

Also present at this election was another Elias Hatfield, a brother of Reverend Anderson Hatfield and a cousin to the Elias who was a brother to Ellison and "Devil Anse." Some

18

time after this, Elias Hatfield (brother of Rev. Hatfield) had bought a fiddle from Tolbert McCoy on which he still owed fifty cents. All of them were drinking and Tolbert attempted to collect the balance due on the fiddle and an argument ensued. Elias Hatfield, when he was drinking, was a very obstinate person and even his brother could not do anything with him, but the McCoys seemed to like the Rev. Anderson Hatfield and would most usually listen to him.

The argument over the fiddle happened about one hundred yards from the beech tree where the election was being conducted. Someone went and told the Rev. Anderson Hatfield that his brother Elias was about to have some trouble with the McCoys and asked him to come down and try to stop it before serious consequences resulted. He went down to the scene of the argument and as usual Elias was under the influence of liquor and would not heed his advice, but the McCoys were persuaded to come up closer to the election grounds and leave Elias alone.

It was a hot day and Ellison Hatfield was lying in the shade of a tree, and having heard of the argument between Elias Hatfield and the McCoys, arose and jestingly offered the McCoys his "Sun-down" straw hat and told them to forget the argument and he would give them the hat to make feed for their cattle. The McCoys were already angry and infuriated so they did not take the offer of the straw hat as a joke in the way Ellison had intended. Having a score to settle with Ellison anyway, Tolbert McCoy walked up to Ellison and

19

Home of the Reverend Anderson Hatfield during his lifetime. This
home is located about two hundred yards from the actual spot where
the feud started on the first Monday in August in the year of 1882.
It is more than one hundred years old and is originally of log structure but has been remodeled in late years. In the foreground is
R. R. Hatfield, an attorney at law, youngest son of Reverend Anderson Hatfield. He has lived in this old homestead more than fifty years.

said, "I'm hell on earth." McCoy drew back seemingly to strike Ellison with his fist but instead he had his knife open in his hand and he stabbed Ellison in the abdomen, cutting him for several inches and severed his liver.

At this instant Ellison struck McCoy with his fist, knocking him down and fell on top of him. McCoy managed to wriggle clear and he and his two brothers stabbed Ellison twenty-five times in the back and then shot him with a revolver injuring him fatally. The Reverend Anderson Hatfield was standing close by and said when McCoy fired he did not see the bullet but saw Ellison's shirt twist when the bullet entered his back.

Ellison was removed by his friends to his home across Tug River about four miles from the scene where he had been wounded. Floyd Hatfield, another brother of the Reverend Anderson Hatfield, being a constable, arrested the three McCoys for the wounding of Ellison. About this time Elias Hatfield (brother of "Devil Anse" and Ellison) rushed up and grabbed Tolbert McCoy by the shirt collar and emptied his revolver in his (McCoy's) face but every shot missed its mark. Observing this strange phenomenon he turned away and remarked, "If that didn't kill you I wouldn't harm a hair on your head."

Floyd Hatfield, the constable, lived about two miles from the scene where the trouble occurred and it was his intention to keep the McCoys at his home that night and the next day

This is the picture of the actual shirt worn by Ellison
Hatfield on the day he was fatally wounded by the Mc-
Coys in 1882. It is an old flax shirt and was made by
the wife of Ellison Hatfield. It is now the property of
Joe Hatfield, son of "Devil Anse."

escort them to the county seat at Pikeville, which was some thirty miles away. It was getting along toward mid-afternoon and their only means of travel being by horseback over the mountain trails, he thought it best to keep the prisoners over-night at his home and take them to jail the next day.

The Reverend Anderson Hatfield, knowing that "Devil Anse," his family and friends would be wrought up over the wounding of his brother and sensing trouble between them and the McCoys, advised his brother Floyd Hatfield, the constable, to proceed to Pikeville that night and avoid any altercation with "Devil Anse," whom he knew would be sure to come as soon as he heard of the trouble in which his brother was wounded, but Floyd, being reluctant to start so far that late in the evening, took a chance on keeping the prisoners overnight at his home. Sure enough, about nightfall "Devil Anse," with several others appeared on the scene, and forcibly taking the prisoners away from the constable, escorted them across the river into West Virginia and kept them under guard day and night in a school house near the home of his brother Ellison.

The Reverend Anderson Hatfield together with some of his friends went to see "Devil Anse" and begged him to release the McCoys and let them be taken on to Pikeville where they could be tried according to law, but he refused, saying, "If my brother Ellison gets well the law can handle it," but not intimating what would happen if Ellison did not recover.

23

The wounding occurred on Monday and Ellison died on Wednesday. The next morning, after the death of Ellison, the three McCoys were found tied to some pawpaw bushes on the Kentucky side of Tug River and all three had been killed.

There were no eye witnesses who would testify that the Hatfields killed the McCoys and on this technicality "Devil Anse" escaped punishment for the killing. (This legal technicality will be fully explained later in this story).

It has been said that these three McCoys were escorted across Tug River and tied to the bushes and told to kneel and pray for they were going to be killed. All of them did so and two were shot to death in that position. The other McCoy being quite young was praying ardently and begging not to be killed and it is rumored that "Devil Anse" was inclined to spare his life, but Jim Vance, being one of those present, walked up to the boy and placed his gun close to the back of his head and fired, blowing out his brains, saying "A dead man tells no tales."

The killing of Ellison Hatfield and the subsequent capture and death of the three McCoys was the actual beginning of West Virginia's and possibly the Nation's most notorious mountain feud. Naturally, Randolf McCoy, the father of the three McCoy boys who were killed while tied to pawpaw bushes was infuriated beyond measure, so he and his friends started gunning for the Hatfields to avenge the death of the boys and the Hatfields were gunning for the McCoys. It

24

This is the scene where the three McCoys, Floyd, Tolbert and Richard, were tied to some pawpaw bushes and killed after the death of Ellison Hatfield whom they had mortally wounded on the memorable election day. The scene is located on the Kentucky side of Tug river just above Matewan, West Virginia.

probably never ocurred to them that to let the law take its course in the matter and settle it in that manner. The uppermost thing in the minds of those on either side was the extermination of the enemy.

In reality, neither the Hatfields nor the McCoys were bloodthirsty people. Both clans were known far and wide for their hospitality and it seemed that they could not do enough for their friends. Before and after these feudal days, a stranger was always welcome in the homes of those on either side and was always extended a glad hand and served at their bountiful tables with pleasure.

It has been said many times of "Devil Anse" that he was the most hospitable host anyone could wish to visit. The latchstring was always on the outside and a glad welcome awaited within where, after having partaken of an unforgetable supper prepared by competent hands over an open fire, they would sit and talk before the firelight of the mountaineer's huge log fire until the wee hours of the morning.

These mountain homes at this time, it must be remembered, were not elaborate homes but they were in most instances happy homes. When these early settlers first migrated to this section, they found only a wilderness in which to establish and build their homes. They could bring very little with them and they had to start from "scratch." Upon reaching the new lands the settler's first concern was to locate a suitable building site. As a rule, the spot chosen was one that could

26

be defended easily and it must be near a water supply, for wells were an unheard of thing in those days.

The settler built his cabin of logs hewed to precision with his keen-bladed axe and covered it with clapboards split from blocks of wood. Sometimes they had no floors, except the ground on which the cabin was built. It would bake hard and serve as an excellent floor. Later floors were made from what was known as puncheons — logs split to the desired thickness and fastened securely by wooden pegs.

Chimneys were usually made from rough stones and topped off with a crib of sticks. Cracks between the logs in the houses were stopped with stones and sticks and like the chimneys were daubed with mortar made from yellow clay.

The inside of the house was almost as simple as the outside. Everything centered about the huge open fireplace which occupied a large part of one end of the building. Pots and kettles hung on hooks and cranes above the fire, and other cooking utensils sat on the broad hearth. A mantel over the fireplace usually held such items as corn-cob pipes, a bottle of brandy and sometimes a picture. Above this mantel hung the trusty rifle, and beside it a shot pouch, hunting bag and powder horn. Nearby on a bench were a water bucket and a wash pan, above which hung a towel and a gourd used for drinking purposes. The spinning wheel and loom were not far away, for the pioneer housewife had to provide clothing material for the family.

27

Hunting, trapping and farming were the chief occupations of these people and corn was their principal crop. An abundant crop of corn made it possible for them to have horses, hogs, cattle and sheep. Horses were used for farming and also for transportation. A sure-footed horse that could get along well over the mountain trails was a prized possession. Cows were kept for their milk and butter supply and hogs made it possible to have good old "hog and hominy."

Even though these people lived a simple life and in crudely constructed cabins, they had an abundent life and most of them were considered good livers.

The home of "Devil Anse" was a favorite stopping place to all those from far and near who knew him, but to those who did not know him personally and had heard of him only as a feudist it was a place to be shunned. Some years after the feud had ended and peace and quiet reigned in the hills once more, a man came to the home of the Reverend Anderson Hatfield selling family Bibles. He stayed all night with him and asked Reverend Hatfield to accompany him for a day or two to see others about his Bibles and he agreed to do so. They started out on their horses and after having gone a ways the salesman made the remark that he wanted to see everyone in that vicinity except "Devil Anse" Hatfield, because from the stories being circulated concerning him and his feudal activities, he thought that anyone coming near enough to him would be shot immediately. He was informed by the Rev. Hatfield that they were on their way to the home of "Devil Anse" and would soon be there. The salesman remonstrated but was finally persuaded to go on. When they arrived at the gate "Devil Anse" appeared in the door to greet them. The salesman sat trembling in his saddle astride his horse but eventually acquired enough courage to dismount and enter the house. They stayed for several hours. Their horses were fed and cared for and they had lunch. The salesman gradually began to lose his sense of fear and seemed to enjoy very much the unexpected hospitality. After they had resumed their journey the salesman remarked that he was never so surprised in his life and that he never enjoyed a visit so much.

During the feudal days it was more or less dangerous for a stranger to be in this section, especially, if he was in the company of or associated with either the Hatfields or Mc-Coys. Even if this particular region was sparsely settled at that time, the movements of almost every one were known to both sides. Scouts for the clansmen were always on watch along the densely wooded hills and a stranger could not get far until he was apprehended by a rugged mountaineer with his ever-ready and trusted rifle. The stranger would be asked to give an account of himself and his business in that area. Sometimes, if he could give a satisfactory reason for being there and could reasonably satisfy the ever-skeptical mind of the scout, he would be allowed to proceed on his journey, at least until he encountered another scout, possibly an enemy of the scout first encountered. On these occasions, if the scout could not be absolutely sure of the authenticity of the stranger's story, he would be asked to return from whence he came and not proceed any farther; or maybe he would be accompanied by the scout to the leader of his clan where he would be dealt with according to the discretion of the leader, who most usually demanded that the stranger leave in the company of a number of clansmen who would escort him out of the area in which they kept an eternal and constant vigil. Even the residents were afraid to get far away from their homes for they never knew when they would be sighted and mistaken for an enemy clansman, whereupon they would be another victim of a rifle bullet fired from ambush.

When from time to time a clansman would be killed in this manner, no one would ever know who fired the shot and for that reason the law was helpless in trying to prosecute the guilty, for no proof could be secured from which to make an indictment, therefore when a clansman would be killed, the other side would increase their efforts to retaliate with "an eye for an eye and a tooth for a tooth."

At frequent intervals during the feud, members on both sides would send a letter or note to the other side saying that a certain one would be killed on a certain date. This naturally kept all parties concerned on the alert and at no time would any feudist on either side let himself be caught unarmed. While plowing in his fields, caring for his stock and even while sleeping, that long barrel rifle was always in reach of his steady hand.

At one time "Devil Anse" was confined in his bed with fever and he received a letter from Harmon McCoy stating that he (Harmon) was coming to kill him. Jim Vance, an active participant in the feud, was at the home of "Devil Anse" when the letter came and he said, "Anse, watch out for him tonight, but if he don't get here tonight you need not be afraid." In a little while Vance left the home of "Devil Anse" supposedly to go for the night to his own home which was not far away, but the next morning Harmon Mc-Coy was found in a cave near the home of "Devil Anse" and he had been killed. No one, of course, knew exactly who killed him, but the McCoys thought they had a pretty good idea.

After having heard of the death of Harmon McCoy and believing that Jim Vance had done the killing, the McCoys started out to get him. A large band of them crossed the river and headed for Vance's house which was located on Thacker Creek. At this time "Cap" Hatfield, the second son of "Devil Anse" was at the home of Vance and they started from Vance's home across the hill to the home of "Cap." They were accompanied by Mary Vance, the wife of Jim. When they reached the top of the hill Mary Vance spied the McCoys coming up the hill and she yelled for

"Cap" and Jim to get under cover at once for the McCoys were not far away. "Cap" asked her how many were in the band and she said it looked as if they were about forty of them.

Jim Vance barricaded himself behind a tree and "Cap" behind a rock just over to the right. By this time the firing had begun and a furious battle ensued for some time. Jim Vance was shot several times in the abdomen, through the tree, and was wounded severely. He told "Cap" to run for his life explaining that he had been mortally wounded. "Devil Anse" at this time was over across another hill on Pigeon Creek with several of his clan. "Cap" sensing his helplessness in facing so many, ran down the hill to Vance's home and went to the barn and jumped astride one of the horses in the barn without even a bridle or saddle and started to find his father and the other clansmen. After "Cap" had ceased firing, the McCoys approached the wounded Vance and finding him not yet dead, they drew their pistols and shot his brains out, then Bud McCoy took some of Vance's brains on his finger and polished his boots with them and then licked his finger.

"Cap" soon reached the place where "Devil Anse" and his men were and they immediately started to the scene of battle, but by the time they arrived it was all over and the McCoys had departed.

"Cap" Hatfield, whose real name was William Anderson

32

Hatfield, having been named after his father, was the right-hand man of "Devil Anse" in all this feud. He was very shrewd and very seldom became excited regardless of the situation which confronted him. By his leadership the Hatfields were led out of many tough spots.

Not long after the battle in which Vance was killed, the McCoys again came across the river and met the Hatfields at the mouth of Grape Vine Creek at the home of "Cap" Hatfield and a tough battle followed. There were thirty-nine of the McCoys and only about six or eight of the Hatfields. The McCoys used a stone wall along the river bank as protection and the Hatfields were behind some old log buildings. Bill Dempsey on the Hatfield side was wounded in the knee and when the Hatfields had to retreat, since they were greatly outnumbered, they had to leave Dempsey behind. Dempsey was lying on the ground in a semi-conscious condition when Jim McCoy and Frank Phillips approached him. He thought it was some of his own friends and asked for a drink of water and Frank Phillips said, "I'll give you water," whereupon he raised his rifle and shot Dempsey in the head, killing him instantly.

After the death of Jim Vance and Bill Dempsey, who were killed by the McCoys, the next thought in the minds of the Hatfields was to avenge their deaths by getting the one who did the killing. They knew that Jim Vance had died at the hands of Bud McCoy and he was their next in-

33

tended victim. He was hunted for several weeks and finally corralled in the home of Randolf McCoy, on Blackberry Fork of Pond Creek in Kentucky. The battle started with the Hatfields surrounding the house and the McCoys on the inside. The Hatfields fired from the cover of bushes and the McCoys from windows and doors, shielding themselves by standing on the side of the openings where they were protected by the heavy logs from which the house was constructed.

The siege lasted far into the night and after dark all the occupants of the house scurried to safety except Calvin McCoy and his sister Alifaire. They remained in the house and kept on firing. Randolf McCoy was in the house when the battle started and he escaped in his night clothes. He carried a double-barrel shotgun and as he ran he wounded one of the Hatfields in the shoulder and shot another's hand off. He went several miles before he stopped and spent the night in a haystack.

The Hatfields, not knowing that the greater part of the McCoys had escaped, decided to set fire to the house and bring them out that way. One of the Hatfields proceeded to the house under the cover of darkness and started a small fire. Alifaire McCoy, sensing the intentions of the Hatfields to burn the house, rushed downstairs and extinguished the blaze with a pitcher of milk. She was spied by the Hatfields and taken for Bud and killed. A few minutes later another

34

fire was started and this time the house began to burn in earnest. Calvin, the only remaining McCoy in the house, knowing that he would be exterminated in the burning house, jumped out of a window and ran for cover of an old barn not far away. He was firing as he ran but just as he was about to reach the security of the barn a bullet struck him in the head, killing him instantly.

Calvin McCoy and his sister Alifaire were buried in the same grave on the hill opposite the old McCoy home place.

At that time Perry Cline was Prosecuting Attorney of Pike County, Kentucky. He had married the daughter of Harmon McCoy and sister of Randolf McCoy, the leader of the feud on the McCoy side. The Hatfields felt that they could not get justice in the Kentucky Courts since Cline was a near relative of the McCoys, and for that reason they tried to elude capture in every way possible. Wall Hatfield and his two sons-in-law were indicted and charged with murder, being among those indicted for murder of the three McCoys on the river bank near Matewan. They had taken no part whatever in the feud and knowing their innocence they had no fear of being convicted and sent word to the Kentucky officers that they would surrender.

They went to Pileville and were put on trial and all were sentenced to life in the penitentiary. Wall Hatfield lived only a short time and died in prison; his two sons-in-law served fourteen years and were pardoned.

This incident proved more than ever to the Hatfields that they had no chance of a fair trial in the Kentucky Courts. They knew positively that these three men had taken no part in the feud and if they were tried and convicted then the ones who had taken an active part in the feud faced an even worse fate at the hands of those whom the Hatfields felt were McCoy sympathizers and who were in a position to get a conviction whether they had evidence of guilt or not. It seemed that all that was necessary to get a conviction was to bring someone to trial whose name was Hatfield or even one who was associated with the Hatfield family.

Ellison Mounts, who was supposed to have been the son of Ellison Hatfield prior to his marriage (he always went by the name of Mounts), was arrested and taken to Pikeville to be tried. Thinking he would receive a lighter sentence, he confessed his part in the feud. He was tried and sentenced to be hanged in the court house yard at Pikeville. After his conviction and before he was hanged he was questioned again about the activities of others in the feud. He refused to give any more information and also stated that he could not tell the same story he had told before and save his own soul.

Johnson Hatfield, the eldest son of "Devil Anse," had been indicted in Kentucky for carrying a pistol, which was an indictable offense under the Kentucky statutes at that

36

time. It has been said that the indictment was a frame-up in order to have a reason to apprehend him. Johnson at that time was courting a girl on the Kentucky side of the river. Jim McCoy, being a constable, and also knowing that Johnson was expected at the home of his girl friend at a certain time, appeared on the scene with several of his brothers and friends and arrested Johnson. They tied him securely with rope and started with him to Pikeville where they intended putting him in jail to await trial on the indictment. In the meantime, the Hatfields had heard that the McCoys had arrested Johnson and knowing the route they would travel with him to Pikeville, gathered their men together, took a shorter route, and waited for them on top of Stringtown Mountain.

When the McCoys reached the top of the mountain with their prisoner, they were surrounded by the Hatfields and were ordered to release Johnson. After having done what they were commanded, they were told to kneel and pray for they were going to be killed. All of them did so except Jim McCoy. He said, "You can shoot me down but I won't get down," whereupon "Devil Anse" called to his men not to fire and said to McCoy, "I admire you for the nerve you have shown." They were then allowed to go on their way.

Johnson was later indicted on seven different counts

in Kentucky for his participation in the feud and also in connection with the burning of Randolf McCoy's home. One day he was apprehended near Cedar, on the West Virginia side of Tug River, kidnapped into Kentucky and taken to Pikeville to await trial.

He received a change of venue from Pike County to Floyd County, where he was tried before Circuit Judge Andy Auxier and Prosecuting Attorney Andy Kirk. He was sentenced to life imprisonment but was later pardoned by Lieutenant-Governor Thorn of Kentucky. J. C. W. Beekham was Governor at the time but refused to give any consideration to the pardon petition for Johnson. Lieutenant-Governor Thorn told them to wait until Governor Beckham was out of the state and he would be acting Governor and would grant the pardon.

Bill Tom Hatfield, a cousin of "Devil Anse" and also an active feudist, was tried in Pikeville and sentenced to prison for life. He served about six years and was pardoned. He lived to a ripe old age and died of natural causes at his home on Tug River only a few years ago.

"Devil Anse" always managed to evade capture, although several rewards were offered for his arrest. He knew that if he were apprehended and taken to Kentucky to stand trial he would be a doomed man. He felt that he would have no chance whatever to get a fair and impartial trial. Upon several occasions he was approached by officers and detectives who wanted to arrest him for the sake of the rewards but he would never consent to go with them. He would tell them that he did not intend to submit to arrest and they knew he meant just what he said. At different times detectives went to his home under pretense of wanting to see him about other matters, thinking they might have an opportunity to arrest him, but he was too hard to fool. They were often invited to eat with him and in some instances they stayed several days as his guests but always left without the object of their mission.

As has been stated, "Devil Anse" lived at Delorme, West Virginia. He owned about five thousand acres of land in that vicinity and also operated a general store. In those days much timber was taken from the dense forests and made into rafts which were floated down the river to the market at Catlettsburg. After disposing of their rafts they loaded push boats with provisions and proceeded back up the river to their homes. This was a long, hard job but it was their only means of getting merchandise for the few country stores. "Devil Anse" used this means of disposing of his timber and restocking his country store for many years.

In those days many of the old settlers made "moonshine" whiskey in their mountain stills. Their principal products were the well known "corn whiskey" made from the corn grown on the mountain farms and "apple brandy" made from the apples grown in their large orchards.

These stills were operated according to law. They obtained government permits to make the whiskey and paid a stipulated tax on each gallon or barrel of whiskey distilled.

Alf Burdette was the principal detective among those who were trying to find someway to effect the arrest of "Devil Anse" in order to receive the rewards. He and Dave Stratton of Delorme, West Virginia, conceived a plan to get "Devil Anse" away from his native haunts, thinking if that could be accomplished they could apprehend him with little effort.

One day Stratton came into the store operated by "Devil Anse" and offered to sell him a calf. They made the deal and Stratton received his money for the calf. Before leaving he asked "Devil Anse" for a drink of whiskey. He was shown a barrel of whiskey in the store and told to drink all he wanted. After this incident Stratton went to Charleston and indicted "Anse" for having in his possession whiskey upon which the tax had not been paid. This was done as a pretense to get "Devil Anse" to Charleston, for they knew he had respect for the Federal law and would answer any summons or indictment which had been returned against him in the Federal Court.

Judge John J. Jackson was then Judge of the Federal Court at Charleston and he knew "Devil Anse" intimately. He surmised the indictment had been made for the purpose of getting "Devil Anse" to come to Charleston where he would be without the protection of his mountain barricades and the constant aid of his fellow clansmen.

40

At that time H. S. White was United States Marshal. He was sent by Judge Jackson to see "Devil Anse" to tell him of the indictment and to ask him to appear for trial on a certain date. "Devil Anse" sent word back to Judge Jackson that he would be glad to come provided he be allowed to bring some of his friends along and that they could come armed, explaining to the judge that he feared trouble with the detectives if he came alone and unarmed. Judge Jackson sent word that he might come as heavily armed as he wished and accompanied by as many men as he wanted.

"Devil Anse" and his men started on their journey to Charleston on horseback, a distance of approximately one hundred miles. They arrived at the specified time and the trial began, but there was no evidence to prove he had whiskey upon which no tax had been paid and the case was dismissed.

The Judge, sensing trouble between the detectives and the Hatfields and also knowing something of how "Devil Anse" was in danger of being taken to Kentucky where he would be at the mercy of those who relentlessly sought his capture so that they might deal with him according to their vengeful desires, told the Marshal to go back home with the Hatfields and if anyone tried to bother "Anse" to arrest them and put them in jail. Therefore, the little trick so cunningly devised by the detectives proved worthless, since it gave them no opportunity to nab their man while he was in Charleston.

41

Finally the Kentucky officials tried to get "Devil Anse" by way of extradition. They made a request of the Governor of Kentucky to have him extradited and the Governor of West Virginia was asked to grant the extradition. According to the West Virginia statutes at that time, the Governor would not honor a request for extradition from another state if the defendant could prove by witnesses that he had not committed a crime in the state that sought his extradition.

Lawyers were scarce at the time and most of those available, fearing the consequences from the opposing side, would have nothing to do with a case for either the Hatfields or McCoys.

After some time the Hatfields secured the services of two young attorneys who lived in Boone County, West Virginia, J. C. Thomas, a school teacher, and Henderson F. Bailey. Both were young and inexperienced but aggressive and intelligent. They rode horseback from their homes in Boone County to the home of "Devil Anse" and made all necessary arrangements to proceed with the case. Then they continued on to Pikeville on their faithful steeds. There they obtained certified copies of the indictments charging "Devil Anse" and about nineteen others with murder. They also obtained the name of the foreman of the grand jury and the name of each juryman, together with the names of the Commonwealth witnesses in the case.

The indictment was endorsed on the back as follows:

42

"The Commonwealth of Kentucky vs. Anderson Hatfield, et al., a felony," and below this the signature of the grand jury foreman making the indictment a "true bill."

All these facts were compiled and brought back by the two young lawyers and a time and place was appointed for a hearing before a justice of the peace in West Virginia, and upon the proof presented by the Commonwealth witnesses named in the indictments of the Kentucky Courts the Governor of West Virginia was to act on the request of extradition.

From the testimony of these Commonwealth witnesses it was proved that there was no evidence whatsoever that the Hatfields had killed the three McCoys. The foreman of the grand jury testified that they had made an indictment against the Hatfields for kidnapping the McCoy boys and taking them to West Virginia, and when the indictments were presented to him for his signature at the end of the session he had signed them without observing that the indictments were for murder instead of kidnapping. The Prosecuting Attorney had changed the findings of the grand jury to murder instead of kidnapping. This was another trick of the McCoy confederate acting as Prosecuting Attorney to get custody of "Devil Anse," because in those days the charge of murder carried a much greater penalty than the charge of kidnapping.

The whole case was then written up by the attorneys and certified by the justice of the peace. Then the papers were taken to the county clerk of Logan County, John Chaffin,

43

who certified to the genuineness of the justice's signature. Afterward these two attorneys filed these papers in the office of Governor Wilson of West Virginia, for his action on the extradition request. After studying all the facts carefully the Governor refused to honor the request for extradition and "Devil Anse" was at last in a manner free, so long as he did not go into Kentucky.

For about sixteen years the Kentucky authorities tried to secure the extradition of "Devil Anse." Each time a new Governor was elected in West Virginia they approached him with a petition asking for the extradition of "Devil Anse," and each Governor, after reviewing the case and noting that his predecessors had refused extradition, acted likewise. Finally the matter was dropped altogether and "Devil Anse" was allowed to live in peace during his remaining years.

He disposed of his property on Tug River and moved to Island Creek where he purchased a large tract of land containing several thousand acres. He remained at this location until his death in 1921.

The following appeared in the Charleston Gazette of January 8, 1921.

"DEVIL ANSE" HATFIELD OF FEUD FAME DIES IN LOGAN COUNTY

CLAN LEADER FALLS VICTIM OF PNEUMONIA
AT AGE OF 82

44

The home of "Devil Anse" Hatfield at the time of his death, located
on Main Island Creek in Logan County. "Devil Anse" moved to
this location some years after the feud ended and built a log home
which was replaced in later years by the above frame structure.

Aged West Virginia Mountain Chieftain Won Nationwide Fame through Bitter Hatfield and McCoy Feud

ALWAYS CARRIED RIFLE WITH HIM

RESPECTED BY JURISTS AND LOVED BY FELLOW NATIVES WHO ARE GATHERING FOR THE FUNERAL

"Devil Anse" Hatfield, leader of the clan in the Hatfield-McCoy feud in the 80's and 90's died at his home on Main Island Creek, Logan County, of a paralytic stroke last Thursday night. Dr. E. R. Hatfield, of this city, a son, left with his family for the old home immediately after receiving word of his father's death.

Though the aged mountain chieftain had been in failing health for several weeks it was an attack of pneumonia which brought about his sudden death, according to information received by his son.

POPULAR IN COMMUNITY

Funeral services will be held at the home at three o'clock Sunday afternoon. Indications are that it will be the biggest funeral in the history of the county, for word from Omar, the nearest town, last night was to the effect that mourning friends from distant points in the mountains already were arriving.

Captain Anderson ("Devil Anse") Hatfield was one of the leaders of the historic feud between the Hatfields and

McCoy families in the mountains of Kentucky and West Virginia. Shot at from ambush and in hand to hand combat with the McCoys scores of times, he had always predicted that he would live to die a natural death, as he now has at the age of 82 without bearing any marks of battle.

"Devil Anse" had a reputation as a crack shot that was known throughout the mountainous region of the two states, and at the age of seventy he could shoot a squirrel out of the tallest timber. He often turned the trick for admirers with the old rifle that he carried ready for action at all hours and with which during the early eighties he would shoot on sight any member of the McCoy family.

The feud lasted for several years and started over the killing of his brother by three of the McCoys in which they stabbed him many times and shot him in the back.

"Devil Anse" had none of the attributes of the "bad man" in his character. He always was recognized as a loyal friend of the many with whom he was acquainted. Numbered among those who believed he had been right by the position he took during the feud were the late Judge John J. Jackson, known as the "Iron Judge" who was appointed to the Federal bench by President Lincoln, and former Governor E. W. Wilson, the former protecting Hatfield from capture when he had been called into court, and the latter refusing to honor a requisition from the Governor of Kentucky, for the arrest of "Devil Anse" on a charge of killing some particular member of the McCoy family.

Hunted by Detectives

Detectives, real and alleged, had aranged for the capture of Hatfield, spurred by a reward, after they had seen to it that he was indicted on a charge of having tax unpaid whiskey in his possession in 1888.

Judge Jackson was on the bench at the time and was informed of the danger that awaited the accused man. Judge Jackson sent word to Hatfield that if he would appear in court without an officer being sent for him, the court would see that he had ample protection until he returned to his home in Logan County.

Hatfield appeared and was acquitted of the charge against him. Some of the detectives pounced upon him soon after he left the court room, but Judge Jackson summoned all of them before him and threatened to put them all in jail, directing special officers to see that Hatfield was permitted to reach his home. After Hatfield was well on his way, Judge Jackson told the detectives that if they wanted their man, they would have to get him just like the McCoys had been trying to do for a number of years. They never went.

Hatfield spent the last fifteen years of his life quietly and peaceably on the farm he owned in Logan County. He raised a good many hogs and other farm products and seldom left the community.

Once he was prevailed upon by some enterprising amusement manager to go on the vaudeville stage. He made all preparations to do so but abandoned the idea when an old indictment was produced which had been quashed on condition that the old mountaineer agree to remain at home the rest of his days.

The Charleston Gazette of January 9, 1921:

HILLMEN FLOCK TO FUNERAL OF
CLAN CHIEFTAN

WHOLE POPULATION OF GUYANDOTTE-BIG SANDY WATERSHED
EXPECTED AT CABIN OF "DEVIL ANSE" HATFIELD TODAY

CIVIL WAR PAL WILL OFFICIATE AT RITES

What promises to be the greatest crowd in the history of the mountains, which form the watershed of the Guyandotte and Big Sandy Rivers, will gather tomorrow at a log homestead on Main Island Creek to pay their last tribute to Captain Anderson Hatfield, a soldier in the Confederacy; "Devil Anse" Hatfield, leader of the Hatfield clan in the famed Hatfield and McCoy feud, and to "Uncle Anse" Hatfield, neighbor and friend, of whom it is said he had fed and sheltered more people than any other man in Logan County.

From Pond Creek in the mountains of Pike County, Kentucky; from the waters of Pigeon, in Mingo; from the borders of McDowell and Mercer, Lincoln, Boone, and Wyoming,

49

the mountaineers are gathering to join with the people of Logan County, as they mourn the passing of the departed chieftain.

The funeral will be held at 3 o'clock, and "Uncle Dike" Garrett, the mountain preacher who served at the side of "Devil Anse" through the Civil War and who later officiated at the baptism of "Devil Anse" and his sons, will be in charge.

The body will be laid to rest in the family graveyard beside those of Troy and Elias, the two sons whose tragic deaths in Fayette County a few years ago occasioned the only break in the family circle before the passing of the patriarch.

The Charleston Gazette of January 10, 1921.

CLAN LEADER LAID TO REST AS
SON ASKS FOR BAPTISM

SEVENTY-FIVE DESCENDANTS SEE BODY
BURIED IN VALE

Only Member of the Family Missing
Is Aged Widow
Too Feeble to Accompany Procession from Cabin

"Devil Anse" Hatfield was laid to rest beside the bodies of his two sons, Troy and Elias, in the family burial ground in a hollow three hundred feet below the crest of the mountain which sheds its water into the Guyandotle on one side and the Big Sandy on the other. The funeral constituted one of the most dramtic scenes in the history of the mountains. There was no funeral sermon. "I'll preach no man's funeral but my own," said "Uncle Dike" Garrett, who as the pastor and friend of Anderson Hatfield, was in charge of the services. But as the pilgrims to this unusual shrine approached the house they were greeted by the sound of singing. Gathered on the porch of the Hatfield home a choir of men and women sang old, old songs, hymns of mourning and of faith with Sim Thompson, famous mountain chorister, as leader. They gathered as they sang around the body, which, enclosed in a golden oak casket lay in state. The people were directed to the porch where they formed in line and passed through the hall that extends from one end of the great house to the other, to view the body.

READY FOR BAPTISM

At the grave "Cap" Hatfield told "Uncle Dike" Garrett that he had made his peace with God and was ready to be baptized whenever the minister said. "I will baptize you, boy," said the old preacher, "in the very hole whar I baptized your pappy."

"Cap" Hatfield raised his hands above his head and declared that he was done with malice and with fighting and that if any man wanted his life or his blood he would not resist.

51

The casket, covered with flowers, was borne around the mountain side by twelve strong-men. Rev. Green McNeely, companion preacher to "Uncle Dike" Garrett who calls him his son in the gospel, spoke a few simple words, not of the dead man, but of the lesson of death, and loosing flowers upon the coffin, now incased in a steel vault, pronounced the words: "Earth to earth, ashes to ashes, dust to dust."

ALL CHILDREN PRESENT

Present at this scene were the eleven surviving children of "Devil Anse," almost all of his forty grand-children and several great grandchildren. There are about seventy-five direct descendants.

The farewell of the widow was taken at the home. At seventy-five she was unable to follow around the mountain after the body of the man with whom she had lived for sixty-one years.

Prayer at the grave was offered by W. A. Robinson, who was a Confederate soldier in the company commanded by Captain Anderson Hatfield. The Island Creek train which bore the funeral contingent from Logan waited at Stirrat, the nearest point to the Hatfield home, until its passengers returned.

The word had gone forth that a patriot had fallen, and in response there was a gathering of the clans. From all directions came men, women and children until thousands had assembled in a spot chosen originally because of inaccessibility in an accessible land. The day was raw and ugly, rain and snow falling alternately while the damp air pierced to the bone.

The crowd followed and stood in the rain during the services. Like those of the house they were unusual as compared with such services outside the mountains. Sid Thompson and his choir sang song after song, old time chants that fell strongly upon the ear of the lowlanders. The old preacher exhorted those about him that they too must shortly go and there was a scene when the family and near relatives gathered to say good-bye to the dead. The casket was opened and an umbrella was held up to keep the rain out of the casket while they said farewell.

This was a bitter fight and it is impossible to get into print or thought every detail of all that happened. It is doubtful if the principal participant could have given a correct account of all the facts, but the foregoing is a brief outline of the principal happenings which has been compiled from data received from reliable sources. It is the intention of the writer to portray mainly the cause which brought about this extended battle between the stalwart mountaineers and also to describe in detail the principal incidents of this far-famed feud in which it is said that twenty-seven people lost their lives. Ellison Hatfield, Jim Vance and Bill Dempsey were the victims on the Hatfield side. The other twenty-four were McCoys and their confederates.

53

Although this was known as the feud between the Hatfields and the McCoys, it does not mean that the feud was a fight between all the Hatfields and all the McCoys. There were many of both names who took no part whatsoever in the feud. Also, many Hatfields felt that the McCoys were right in their feudal activities and many McCoys felt that the Hatfields were right.

The happy thought of today is that many descendants of both sides have entirely forgotten the old trouble between their fore-parents and the matter is seldom mentioned any more.

Many of the descendants of both factions still live in the section of Kentucky and West Virginia along Tug River and have married into each other's families. Let us hope that there will never again be a recurrence of this vindictive monstrosity.

The End.

Monument erected to the grave of "Devil Anse" Hatfield at a cost of more than three thousand dollars.

55

THE STORY OF SID HATFIELD
AND THE
MATEWAN TRAGEDY

SID HATFIELD
at the time he was chief of police of
Matewan, W. Va.

THE STORY OF SID HATFIELD
AND THE
MATEWAN TRAGEDY

NOTE: *The following story of Sid Hatfield and the Matewan Tragedy happened more than thirty years after the end of the feud between the Hatfields and McCoys and had no connection whatever with the famous old mountain feud.*

W E have had wars from the beginning of time. Wars
between nations. Wars between peoples of the same
nation. Revolutionary wars; civil wars; intermingled
conflicts between political and economic factions, disputes between labor and capitalism, employer and employee. These
conditions always have and always will bring about a state
of grief, misery and chaos.

Three hundred years ago when the Indians roamed the
wilds of Mingo County on Tug River along the borders of
Kentucky and West Virginia, Tribal wars existed. Indian
Chieftans ruled with an ironclad hand. He and his tribe
protected their "squaws" and "papooses" by a unified defense
and provided them with the spoils of war. Just as every other
war is made cruel by its casualties when men fight and die for

the cause in which they believe, so were the wars of the Mingo County Indian tribes.

Being Indians, they thrived on the Indian mode of living and with them there was as little to fear from under the ground as there was from overhead. The "Redmen" knew, perhaps, that burried under Mingo County were "black nuggets" of unlimited number which were placed there by the same hand that gave to Mingo County its picturesque beauty, but it took a later American, with that kind of American ingenuity that has transformed the United States from a vast wilderness in 1776 to the leading world power today, to take these "black nuggets" and develop them into an industry of unestimated wealth.

Today, industrially and financially, Mingo County and coal are synonymous. Coal, directly and indirectly, provides for the Mingo County citizens much of their contentment, happiness and prosperity. To remove the coal mining industry from Mingo County would be to cut its very life-line of existence.

The development of this great industry was, of course, slow at first when men of limited resources laid the groundwork for what later began to attract the attention of the nation's leading capitalists and industrialists. Railroads had to be built; modern machinery and equipment had to be put into use. Fields and forests were transformed into thriving communities. Churches and schools were organized, and today in Mingo

60

County many thousands of men go down into the pits or back under the mountains to earn their living and provide for the welfare of their families.

During the years of 1918 and 1919 the coal miners of Mingo County started their drive to organize the miners in this field and affiliate with the United Mineworkers of America. This movement was, of course, protested and resented by the mine owners and coal operators. Most usually when a miner would join the union he would be discharged by his employer and asked to vacate the house in which he lived. Some of the men would comply with this request and others would refuse and defy the rights of their employers to dispossess them. In many instances when miners would refuse to vacate company houses the mine owners would request their dispossession by legal process.

Usually the law enforcement officers were life-long natives of this section, many of them having close friends and relatives that were miners; therefore it can be understood that they would be reluctant to take any active part in the eviction of miners from their homes upon request of the mine owners because the miners had joined the union. This does not mean, however, that they were lax in the enforcement of the law or in the performance of their duty, but they felt that it would be best if they remained neutral and not take any part at all in a conflict which they were foresighted enough to see was inevitable.

61

At this time Sid Hatfield was Chief of Police at Matewan, West Virginia, a thriving picturesque mountain town in Mingo County, nine miles east of Williamson, West Virginia, on Tug River.

Sid Hatfield was born and reared on Blackberry Creek, in Pike County, Kentucky, near the West Virginia border. He was the son of Jacob and Rebecca Hatfield, who were of the pioneer family of Hatfields of this section. His youth was typical of that of other mountain boys. He received a limited education in the public schools of Pike County and at an early age started working alongside his several brothers in the coal mines. He was always considered to be peaceable and was well-liked by all who knew him.

Having been a coal miner most of his life, he understood the miners' problems and when they began their struggle to unionize, to protect their rights and better their working conditions, he naturally was sympathetic toward their undertakings and more or less became one of their leaders. Even though he had become Chief of Police at Matewan he still considered the miners his best friends and their troubles became his troubles. The greater portion of these miners were natives of this section, and the mining industry had given to them the opportunity to earn a livelihood, but yet they felt they had a right to form their own organization which would enable them to have a voice in matters concerning their working regulations and conditions.

62

Not only in and around Matewan but throughout the entire Mingo field the miners began to join the union in great numbers during the early part of 1920. The employees of one particular company near Matewan started a movement to organize, and to offset this movement this company discharged several of the employees and ordered them to vacate the houses in which they lived. The company secured ejectment warrants to dispossess the employees and their families from their homes and employed detectives to execute the warrants and make the evictions.

On May 19, 1920, about twelve or thirteen Baldwin Felts detectives came to Matewan on an early train to serve these eviction warrants. They were heavily armed and upon their arrival proceeded to the place where they were to evict employees of the company that had secured their services. Several hours later, after having made the evictions, they came back to Matewan and went to a local hotel to get supper before boarding a train for Bluefield, W. Va., which was due to arrive there about 5:15 p. m.

During the day the news of what was taking place had spread over the entire community. Nothing was said of any intended reaction on the part of the miners but one could detect a feeling of strained tenseness in the air. The average miner is not a talkative person and no word was passed around that would give a hint of a catastrophe being in the offing. Small groups of miners were milling about the little town, which is the usual scene in a mining community.

63

The Mayor of Matewan, C. C. Testerman, owned a jewelry store directly opposite the Norfolk & Western Depot, about one block from the hotel at which the detectives had gone for supper.

It is said that when the detectives left the hotel they started toward the depot, supposedly to board the train, but on their way they encountered Mr. Testerman, the Mayor, and Sid Hatfield, Chief of Police, standing in front of Testerman's jewelry store. Albert Felts approached Mayor Testerman and explained that he had a warrant for the Town Marshal, Sid Hatfield, charging him with interfering with one of the Baldwin-Felts men while they were arresting a union mine organizer. The Mayor told Felts that the warrant was a "bogus one" and he could not spare Hatfield from the town, but offered to try him as ex-officio justice of the peace, and ask for a bond. The miners say that Felts did not speak a word but shot the Mayor five times with an automatic which was in his pocket. The bullets took effect in Mayor Testerman's abdomen and he died seven hours later in a Welch, West Virginia, hospital. It was said that before Felts made another move he was shot in the head by Sid Hatfield. General firing started from several different directions and in two minutes ten men were dead and five wounded. The shooting occurred in the open and the detectives were plain targets as well as the miners.

In his defense Hatfield said that he did not interfere with the Baldwin guard in his attempt to arrest a union organizer.

He said a crippled union organizer made several speeches at Matewan and vicinity and that he was arrested and placed on a Williamson train. One of the organizer's friends told him to get off the train, that the guard had no authority to arrest him, and he walked off the train unmolested by the guard.

Seven of the detectives were killed outright; two of them swam the river and escaped through the hills of Kentucky; two escaped on the train which had arrived at the station during the shooting, and another was supposed to have been shot from the bridge as he attempted to cross into Kentucky. It was learned, however, that he finally arrived safely at Bluefield, W. Va., but had been wounded.

All five shots fired at Mayor Testerman took effect in his abdomen. The other two men killed were "Tot" Tinsley and Bob Mullens, both miners. Tinsley took no part in the shooting whatever. He was only a bystander, but a stray bullet found its mark in his head.

Mullens was an active participant in the shooting. He was pursued around the corner of the bank by one of the detectives. The detective waited at one window of the bank and as Mullens passed the window on the other side of the bank the detective fired at him through both windows killing him instantly. Neither window of the bank was shattered. The bullet passed through both windows creating a hole just large enough to permit its passing but did not shatter the glass.

The bodies of the detectives lay in the streets for more

65

than two hours until the arrival of the sheriff of Mingo County from Williamson, nine miles away. The miners then assisted the sheriff in picking up the bodies and placing them in a baggage car in which they were transported to Williamson undertaking establishments.

The next day after the Matewan tragedy one of the detectives was in the hospital at Bluefield recovering from the wounds he received in the fracas and he gave the following story of the shooting:

"After making arrangements with the county authorities in a manner satisfactory to their wishes in the matter of issuing writs of eviction and then finding the officers unwilling to perform their duty under the law, twelve of our men proceeded to Matewan yesterday morning to serve eviction papers on miners who had been requested by one of the mine owners to vacate their houses. The evictions were peaceably accomplished and six families were removed from the houses of the coal corporation. Upon request we assisted in moving the furniture of one woman from one of the houses. Apparently everything was done in a peaceable and satisfactory manner according to law. After completing our mission we went our way smiling and joking with friends in the mining community.

We went to the hotel for supper, and some of us having no pistol licenses, we all placed our rifles in suit cases. After

This picture shows a portion of the town of Matewan, W. Va.
Opposite the Norfolk & Western depot is the scene where ten men
were killed and five wounded on the day of the Matewan tragedy.

supper we started to the station to catch the train. Near the station Albert Felts was approached by a little short man that I didn't know. A small crowd gathered. Mr. Felts said: "Let's walk down this way." They walked to a nearby store door and Mr. Felts held a paper which he had taken from his pocket in both hands. He was facing the inside of the store. The little fellow stepped back inside and shots were fired from within at close range striking Mr. Felts in the face. He crumpled over and fell instantly dead.

"Immediately shots came from many windows and corners, and the volleys continued for about fifteen minutes. Undoubtedly over a hundred men were armed and shooting at the twelve of us scattered about the station with no guns. My brother and I jumped the fence and ran into a vacant house which we found occupied by men with rifles and revolvers. I received my shoulder wounds there, but we managed to escape to the next house where no one was at home. When the train pulled in we managed to escape in time to board the last car and were not again discovered."

A short time after this shooting occurred a special session of the Grand Jury was called and Sid Hatfield and twenty-three others were indicted for the killing of the detectives. Later at a trial in the Mingo Circuit court they were acquitted and set free.

Some time afterward, Sid Hatfield married the widow of

Mayor Testerman who was killed on the day of the shooting, and the jewelry store which was operated by Testerman was converted into a hardware store. Hatfield was later elected as constable of Magnolia District which comprised the town of Matewan and other adjacent mining communities.

The Matewan tragedy by no means was the end of the trouble in the Mingo field over the miners desire to organize. In many other localities trouble broke out between mine guards and miners in which many killings resulted. The evicition of families from mine property became so numerous that finally tent colonies sprang up overnight and several thousand miners and their families lived in these tent cities. They were determined not to be outdone but at times their chances for a union organization and peace with the mine operators looked very slim. The operators steadfastly refused to recognize the union men, and in turn the men were just as obstinate in meeting the demands of the operators to work in the mines without belonging to the union.

After Sid Hatfield became so prominent a figure in the Matewan affair he was never left out of the spotlight and was most always accused of being a party to, or a participant in, each of the skirmishes of the succeeding months.

The mine operators and the mine guards considered him to be a sympathizer with, and the leader of, the miners, and whether or not he was active in various gun battles did not alter their belief that he was more or less behind every altercation, although they were never able to get any direct proof that he actually participated.

Some time after he had been acquitted of the Matewan shooting in the Mingo Circuit court, there was a severe battle between mine guards and miners at Mohawk, West Virginia, a small village in McDowell County, and Sid was accused of taking part in the affair, and was indicted by the McDowell County Grand Jury. At that time W. J. (Bill) Hatfield, a distant relative of Sid Hatfield, was sheriff of McDowell County. He came to Matewan with a Warrant for the arrest of Sid and one other man accused of being an accomplice in the shooting. The other man was Ed Chambers, who had been a deputy under Sid and figured prominently with him in the Matewan affair. They were both arrested and taken to Welch, West Virginia, for a preliminary hearing.

Sid spent one night in the McDowell County jail, due to the absence of the judge of the county, but the next day he and Chambers gave bond and returned to their homes in Matewan to await trial in Circuit Court.

On the morning of August 2, 1921, Sid Hatfield and Ed Chambers, together with their wives boarded an early train at Matewan on their way to Welch, W. Va. This was the day on which their trial was to begin. They arrived at Welch at about nine o'clock and since they were not to appear at the court house until 10:30 A. M. they went directly to a local hotel and later to the office of their attorney. At the ap-

70

pointed hour they left their attorney's office and proceeded to the court house so as to be on time for the trail. Leading from the street to the court house there is a long flight of almost perpendicular steps up to the level of the court house. Hatfield and Chambers with their wives climbed these steps and just as they reached the top of the steps there was an instant volley of shots and when the smoke cleared away Hatfield and Chambers both lay dead. The true story of just how Hatfield and Chambers met their deaths or who fired the shots that killed them will, in all probability, remain a mystery. Out of a jumble of conflicting reports, contrasting statements and contradictory rumors there were, of course, accusations, and indictments were made but no convictions were ever obtained against anyone for the killing of the two men.

Thus ended the career of Sid Hatfield who at the age of twenty-nine years had in the past year of his life became a picturesque figure in the industrial life of Mingo County and was known as the "mightiest of two-gun men, terror of Mingo County, and champion of the union mining faction," but today amid the roar of "six-guns" and with the smoke of powder eddying around him he had met his death.

The wives of Hatfield and Chambers stated that they were both unarmed and possibly they thought this to be true, but after the battle a .38 caliber revolver from which four shots had been fired was found beside the body of Chambers.

71

Beside the body of Hatfield who lay sprawled in death on the walk still wearing his familiar smile was found a .38 caliber revolver which had been emptied and in his pocket was another revolver of the same caliber.

Later that day the bodies of Hatfield and Chambers encased in two rough boxes were returned to their homes in Matewan in the baggage car of a Norfolk & Western train. Two coaches to the rear were the two grief-stricken widows. Between fresh outbreaks of tears they were reviewing in memory, the events of the day in which each saw her husband fall in death.

On the day of the funeral many thousands gathered in the little town of Matewan to view for the last time the bodies of Hatfield and Chambers who were considered by the miners and hill-folk as heroes and martyrs.

It rained several times during the morning and violently just about one o'clock at the time when the funeral procession was to be formed. When the rain stopped the bearers started from the humble home of Ed Chambers down the main street on the long walk to the grave. They passed, bearing the casket, a massive metal affair, between lines of Redmen, Pythians and Odd Fellows, halting in front of the Testerman building, several squares down the main street, while the body of Hatfield, incased in a yet more massive casket, was borne to the street by his brother Knights of Pythians. Then with

the two caskets at the head, the long procession moved, passing
down across the trestle beneath which the turgid waters of
swollen Mate Creek raged, and on to the foot bridge which
leads across Tug river to the cemetery at Buskirk, Kentucky,
directly opposite Matewan, W. Va. The strong wire structure
swayed and waved beneath the foot of crowds who hurried
across in front of the funeral march.

It sagged beneath the weight of the caskets as they were
borne across it one at a time. The body of Hatfield was in
the lead followed closely by Mrs. Hatfield and her immediate
relatives, then came the Chambers cortege, with the young
widow who had stood firmly beside her husband when he
was shot down being led by her two brothers.

At the grave the clouds poured out their grief in torrential
tears as the crowds passed through the narrow space between
the two caskets and the simple mountain services were conducted. Mrs. Hatfield was at the head of her husband's casket
crying out to him of her love and sorrow. "I'll never forget
you, my sweetheart," she sobbed as the minister read from
the 133th chapter of Corrinthians and offered a touching
prayer.

The body of Sid Hatfield was committed to the ground
by the Knights of Pythias, and that of Chambers by the
Independent Order of Redmen. The Odd Fellows were also
in attendance honoring the dead chief of police, who was a
member of their order. The grand keeper of seals and records

for West Virginia Pythians spoke in behalf of the three orders. He recited the cardinal virtues for which these orders stand and declared that such principals usually represented good citizenship, men standing for law and order, and not for the rule of strong armed might.

The End

Scene on Tug River looking east from Matewan, W. Va., showing
the picturesque beauty of the mountains in this section. On one side
of the river are the mountains of West Virginia and on the other side
the hills of Kentucky.

COSIMO is a specialty publisher of books and publications that inspire, inform, and engage readers. Our mission is to offer unique books to niche audiences around the world.

COSIMO BOOKS publishes books and publications for innovative authors, nonprofit organizations, and businesses. **COSIMO BOOKS** specializes in bringing books back into print, publishing new books quickly and effectively, and making these publications available to readers around the world.

COSIMO CLASSICS offers a collection of distinctive titles by the great authors and thinkers throughout the ages. At **COSIMO CLASSICS** timeless works find new life as affordable books, covering a variety of subjects including: Business, Economics, History, Personal Development, Philosophy, Religion & Spirituality, and much more!

COSIMO REPORTS publishes public reports that affect your world, from global trends to the economy, and from health to geopolitics.

FOR MORE INFORMATION CONTACT US AT
INFO@COSIMOBOOKS.COM

➢ if you are a book lover interested in our current catalog of books

➢ if you represent a bookstore, book club, or anyone else interested in special discounts for bulk purchases

➢ if you are an author who wants to get published

➢ if you represent an organization or business seeking to publish books and other publications for your members, donors, or customers.

**COSIMO BOOKS ARE ALWAYS
AVAILABLE AT ONLINE BOOKSTORES**

VISIT COSIMOBOOKS.COM
BE INSPIRED, BE INFORMED

CPSIA information can be obtained
at www.ICGtesting.com
Printed in the USA
BVHW082148170322
631641BV00003B/485